MAKING ARCHITECTURE
The Getty Center

MAKING ARCHITECTURE
The Getty Center

Harold M. Williams
Ada Louise Huxtable
Stephen D. Rountree
Richard Meier

Thames and Hudson

Since the publication of *The Getty Center: Design Process* in 1991, and with the move to the new Getty Center in 1997, some of the names of the Getty's programs and institutes have changed. The J. Paul Getty Museum is now The J. Paul Getty Museum at the Getty Villa and The J. Paul Getty Museum at The Getty Center. The Getty Center for the History of Art and the Humanities is now The Getty Research Institute for the History of Art and the Humanities. The Getty Art History Information Project is now The Getty Information Institute. The Getty Center for Education in the Arts is now The Getty Education Institute for the Arts. The Museum Management Institute is now The Getty Leadership Institute for Museum Management.

First Published in Great Britain in 1997
by Thames and Hudson Ltd, London

©1997 THE J. PAUL GETTY TRUST
1200 Getty Center Drive, Suite 400
Los Angeles, California 90049

British Library Cataloguing-in-Publication Data
A catalogue record for this book is available from the British Library

ISBN 0-500-280320

Printed and bound in United States of America

CONTENTS

INTRODUCTION   Harold M. Williams

This publication marks the completion of a fourteen-year project to plan, design, build, and occupy the Getty Center. I have had the privilege of being both an involved principal in and an awed witness to the simultaneous shaping of the complex and the programs of the Getty that would occupy it. That the design of the structures and the character of the programs inhabiting them would develop concurrently was a singular feature of this architectural undertaking. To me, the Getty Center represents a triumph of that most creative and most challenging process.

I am reminded of a quote by Winston Churchill: "We shape our buildings; thereafter they shape us." The programs of the Getty and the architecture of the Getty Center are even more inextricably linked. The process of shaping the programs influenced the design of the Center; the intellectual exercise of designing the Center worked synergetically to determine the nature of our programs. Building from the inside out necessitated asking basic questions: What do we want to accomplish with our programs? How will the buildings support the programs they serve? What will the built environment be like and how will it relate to the natural environment? Our pursuit of answers to these and other questions was central in defining the Getty's mission and the scope of its activities in the understanding, enjoyment, and preservation of the world's artistic and cultural heritage. By making architecture, we created an institution with an extended reach and deep local roots, inwardly turned and outward looking, with a sense of permanence and a predilection for change.

In committing ourselves to build the Getty Center, we believed in the potential for architecture to nurture a diverse professional community, display works of art in a powerfully affecting way, and uplift the general public and staff alike. We wanted the Getty Center to be timeless and a work of art in itself, because, to the outside world, the Getty Center makes a statement about what the Getty is at its core. This was our vision in 1983, when we embarked on this enterprise. Thanks to our architect, Richard Meier & Partners; our contractor, Dinwiddie; a host of consultants; the Getty staff; and the community, this is precisely what we are experiencing in 1997.

In reviewing what transpired to make that vision this reality, I must acknowledge Richard Meier's extraordinary passion for and dedication to this work over many, many years. His design has given us structures that serve and support our mission on several levels. The structures set an example of enduring artistic quality. They communicate both the unity and commonality of our broad purposes here, as well as the distinctive differences in points of view and specific functions, and they serve those functions well. Beyond all of that, they provide an inspiring setting for experiencing and understanding art. I thank him and his colleagues for listening so well, for enlightening us, and for allowing us to educate them as well.

I must also make special mention of three people who breathed life into the Getty Center. Steve Rountree, director of operations and planning, not only brought the building program to fruition and influenced its design, but also worked closely with community leaders and was the point person for Getty staff needs and concerns. Michael Palladino, the design partner at Richard Meier & Partners' Los Angeles office, was responsible for the day-to-day interaction between architect and client. Curt Williams, director of construction, handled the complexities of the daily contractor-architect relationship. The Getty owes a deep debt of gratitude to this tireless triumvirate.

Here, then, is the book documenting the process that has brought us to this day, readying the Getty Center for its public opening. Mirroring the nature of the architecture itself, the points of view expressed here are numerous and highly subjective. A multitude of voices is heard through essays, a number of perspectives seen through photographs, a variety of visions glimpsed through sketches and drawings.

Just as the process of its creation evokes different interpretations from those who helped shape it, the Getty Center now represents different things to those who come in contact with it. To Los Angeles, the Center is an investment in the future of this exciting, polyglot city. It is a major cultural force and participant on all levels in the city's activities. To the Getty staff, views to the city, specifically framed by the architecture, constantly remind them to whom they are responsible: the community at large. The setting challenges and inspires staff, providing a locus in which to exercise their imagination and artistic vision. The very nature of the site and the architecture of the Getty Center inspires us in our mission, reminding us of our exceptional commitment to the field and to making a difference.

For me, my office was among the first to move here—in August, 1996—and I experience deep pleasure on my daily walks around the Center. There's a beauty and a subtlety and an excitement about it, a blending of building, landscape, and views that is extraordinary. In addition to reveling in the aesthetics, I witness the staff interacting on a casual basis—at the espresso cart, on the tram, in the Cafe—which affirms our original vision of collaboration among the programs. This was our primary motivation in building the Getty Center...and it is happening.

Buildings sometimes act as containers to hold back change. I know that by the feel and nature of its architecture, the Getty Center embodies permanence. On the other hand, with its dynamism and complexity, I trust the Getty Center will always be in and of the moment, encouraging growth and change in all who visit and work here.

1982
The J. Paul Getty Trust purchases Los Angeles hilltop site for the Getty Center.

1983
October
Getty invites thirty-three architects to submit qualifications for consideration as Center's architect.
November
Architect Selection Committee chooses seven semifinalists.

1984

August
Stephen D. Rountree named as director
of Getty building program.
Richard Meier selected as project architect.
November
First meeting of Getty Planning Committee.

1985

March
Los Angeles Planning Commission grants use
permit to Getty Center, establishing broad planning
and operational parameters.
February–June
Getty staff and architects visit museum sites
in United States, Canada, and Europe.

1986

March
Getty delivers architectural program
to Richard Meier & Partners and consultants.
April
First meeting of Design Advisory Committee,
Richard Meier & Partners, and Getty staff.
September
Richard Meier & Partners opens Los Angeles office.

1987

February
Dinwiddie Construction Company selected
as project general contractor.
August
Site master plan approved by Los Angeles
Planning Commission.
September
Dinwiddie begins to prepare site for construction.

1988

January
Getty selects automated tram as
transportation system between parking structure
and Center buildings.
September
Getty approves schematic design of Center.

1989

June
Thierry Despont hired to design interiors
of Decorative Arts galleries in collaboration with
curator Gillian Wilson.

November
Construction at Lower Parking facility begins.

1990

January
Representatives from Getty,
Richard Meier & Partners, and Dinwiddie
visit stone quarries in Italy.

May
Grading for main complex of buildings begins.
Getty approves Richard Meier & Partners'
selection of Italian travertine stone as cladding,
in combination with metal panels.

1991

March
Los Angeles Planning Commission
grants final design approval for Center.

April
Getty approves Center design.

October
Getty Center design unveiled to public.

December
Planting of hills with 3,000 California Oaks begins.

1992

June
Foundation work on North Building, East Building, Auditorium, and Restaurant/Cafe begins.
Getty selects California artist Robert Irwin to design Central Garden.

October
Foundation work for Museum building begins.

1993

August
First travertine stone piece set in East Building.
Erection of structural steel for East and North Buildings begins.

November
Olin Partnership begins association with Richard Meier & Partners as landscape architects.
Erection of structural steel for Auditorium begins.

1994

January
Northridge earthquake: structural steel work halted due to concerns raised in earthquake's aftermath; studies undertaken to address concerns.

May
Thierry Despont, in collaboration with Museum staff and Richard Meier & Partners, begins selection of finishes for the galleries. Retrofitting of erected steel joints, identified after Northridge earthquake as vulnerable, begins.

August
Foundation work for Research Institute building begins.
Retrofitting of steel joints completed.
Erection of structural steel for Museum building begins.

December
Parking structure and tram station completed.

1995

April
Getty approves Robert Irwin's design for Central Garden.

July
Erection of structural steel for Research Institute building begins.

1996

January
Construction of Central Garden begins.

June
Security, Facilities, Information Technology staffs move to Getty Center.

July
Conservation Institute staff moves into East Building.

August
Education Institute and Grant Program staffs move into East Building.
Trust Administration staff moves into North Building.
Cafe opens.

September
First meeting of Trustees in Getty Center Board Room.

1997

February
Museum begins staff move and gallery installation.

April
Research Institute begins collections installation.

June
Research Institute begins staff move.

July
Information Institute staff moves into North Building.

November
Construction of Central Garden completed.

December
Public opening of the Getty Center.

THE CLASH OF SYMBOLS   Ada Louise Huxtable

The critic Colin Davies tells us that we live in a world of meaning where architecture conveys the messages. Nowhere is this more evident than at the Getty Center. Architecture keeps no secrets. It is the great communicator. It tells us everything we need to know, and more, about those who conceive and build the structures that define our cities and our time. We sense instantly whether their vision was mean or grand: whether they felt responsible only to themselves and the bottom line or to a larger idea of society and the world. Above all, buildings tell us how their sponsors want to be perceived in the public eye.

A group of buildings of distinctive character, like the Getty Center, interacting with a spectacular hilltop site, sends a particularly powerful message. It creates an image—in this case a major and unforgettable one—that describes the client truthfully and unsparingly; objectives, ideals, tastes, and standards are fully revealed by the architect chosen and the style and quality of the result. The message is delivered with all this information encoded.

Like all communication, that message can be read in more than one way; how it is received depends on the receptors and the attitudes of the viewer.

For some, the immediate effect of the Getty Center is positive, even exhilarating—it is hard not to react to the magic of a "city on a hill"; there is no culture that has not placed its best buildings high, that has not directed its ambitions to the sky. The Center's critics—they come with the territory and are present from the start—see only a monument at a time when monuments are out of favor; the wall visible from the freeway below is "exclusionary," the elegance of the architecture "elitist," and the Getty agenda of education, conservation, research, and scholarship in the arts "paternalistic." The politically correct clichés of the moment come easily and will probably die hard. For many, however, this kind of building, in Davies's astute definition, represents "a vigorous commitment to a program or principle," carried out in "top-drawer architecture." The Getty, and its architecture, take the long view of its mission and expression.

To understand anything as complex as the Getty Center requires some knowledge of the personalities and philosophies involved, and how the product evolved. While a basic design idea was established and held from the start, it was shaped by an unending series of constraints and conditions that profoundly influenced the final result. Zoning restrictions, seismic codes, soil conditions, neighborhood concerns, and many invisible factors required constant conceptual and design revisions. In this way, ideas were

tested and clarified, their expression refined and strengthened. The Getty's programs were actually being developed at the same time as the architect's solutions (talk about architecture as process!). An important part of the story is told in Stephen D. Rountree's essay; he explains—as one example—how the Research Institute for the History of Art and the Humanities was totally redesigned to make its newly defined and still fluid philosophy and practices operative in the building. In another example, the main entrance area became a large, paved platform because a strategic place was needed for fire trucks to turn around; this was translated into an Arrival Plaza that also serves as a primary social space and a location for special activities.

There was no preset scheme or formula, no preconceived Beaux Arts or City Beautiful model of access or procession. Much was fortuitous and serendipitous. A great deal was agonizing hard work. Site models proliferated. Details became full-scale mockups. Plans were submitted and resubmitted to authorities and neighborhood groups. Revisions were made each time that led gradually—and sometimes painfully—to a stronger and more expressively unified concept. At every step, not just the buildings were involved; their integration with the site to preserve and exploit its unique beauty was always a priority.

A project this demanding—multilayered and many-faceted, with so many activities and institutions—does not spring, Minerva-like, from the architect's head as a pure and unadulterated explosion of style and self-expression. What may look like formalism because of the ordered solutions was an organic process, elegantly resolved. There is much to be factored into any assessment of the result.

The message of the architecture is not revealed at first sight. The buildings that form the wall along the perimeter of the hill conceal a campuslike arrangement of carefully related structures that is not apparent until one arrives at the top. Disposing the buildings peripherally in this fashion instead of filling the ravine at the middle of the site was the first major decision; this opens that dramatic natural formation for the landscaping and gardens that are so central to the project, and so integral to the visitor's total experience.

By any measure, this is an extraordinary experience, offering exceptional pleasures: the magnificent, far vistas of Los Angeles and the Pacific, interacting with controlled, near views as one moves through and between buildings and along the outdoor walkways that emphasize the beauty of the setting through the processional and framing devices of architecture. Everywhere, there are subtly calculated and often unexpected viewing points that turn one's attention to the city and the ocean, in the context of the buildings themselves. Construction that seems massive on completion is soon gentled by the lush plantings that take over in true California style.

Is the Getty style California style? And what do we mean by California style? Again, the answer is in how one chooses to perceive and comprehend it. California style, as it is understood and being practiced today by some talented California architects, is pushing the frontiers of architecture in a particularly California way. If there is an avant-garde, it is here; this is a style full of dramatic sculptural shapes and colors and an exuberant manipulation of advanced technology. It combines an edgy California chic with profound architectural investigations of form and space. Led by the influential Frank Gehry, it includes the work of such younger practitioners as Thom Mayne, Eric Moss, and the late Frank Israel. The freedom and the desire to explore are in unique supply on the West Coast, infused with a spirit that is equally a product of the legendary California lifestyle and popular California mythology; this is the place where styles start and move from west to east.

But there is also history here; the work of Frank Lloyd Wright, of expatriate early modernists Richard Neutra and Irving Gill, fits the landscape like a glove. The stark white geometries of the transplanted International Style, given new modulation and meaning by the California sun, have been absorbed in a particularly felicitous fashion into the local mainstream. Meier's design for the Getty fits the landscape in the same way; it is an exemplar of the classic, reductive, minimalist, modernist manner, refined and carried forward, at home in the California tradition.

An institution with the gravitas and resources of the Getty Trust seeks an image that is timeless rather than trendy, in the most relevant and lasting idiom of the architecture of its own time. Something more on-the-edge would be neither representative nor acceptable to a community aggressively unsympathetic to any kind of architectural domination. The Getty does not masquerade as part of the counterculture; it is devoted to the preservation and propagation of the best that civilization has to offer. It is in the business of recording and preserving, of finding ways to make the uses and pleasures of the arts available where opportunities have ceased to exist. Meier's architecture clearly matches that image and intent.

Should there be anything to debate about this architecture if its messages of beauty, utility, and suitability are so clear? Again, it depends on how one perceives the Getty Trust—as a pioneering activist in its outreach programs or as a representative of the status quo. Neither its educational mission, intended to reach all levels in the nation's arts-starved schools, nor its funding of conservation efforts for an endangered international heritage, nor its promotion of scholarship through research and study grants has received the same publicity as the costs of the complex and the amount of Getty funds expended on it, which has been far better tracked by the press than its philanthropic purposes. Construction has been treated like an episode of the TV series on the homes of the rich and famous with that same touch of voyeurism, envy, and censure that gives the perennially popular program its particular kick.

In this case, however, voyeurism is not the end of it; the public is invited—the cost of entry is a parking ticket. For the same fee charged at the Los Angeles beaches used by an overwhelming mix of color, class, and ethnic populations, as many as can fit into a private or public vehicle will be free to roam the site, enjoy the views and gardens, visit the Museum, attend programs, or just make a day of it in L.A. style. There are concerned observers who would have preferred to see the

money spent in the inner city, who find a disconnect between the Getty and the community because of its hilltop location in an exclusive neighborhood. It is worth noting that this glorious site, now open to all, would otherwise be publicly inaccessible. The tram ride up the hill to the top is much like the Pompidou Center's popular exterior elevators to the rooftop view of Paris; destination is everything. Many never enter the museum there but take the ride for its own sake. Like the present Museum at Malibu, the Getty Center is meant for public use and pleasure.

However, no one expected another Roman villa. The classicism of the Malibu Museum, derided at first, has turned it into the kind of appealingly faux artifact dearly beloved by all; it has taken its place comfortably in an adaptable and forgiving landscape. It has become its own thing—a California-Italy, Pacific Ocean-Bay of Naples hybrid—with a unique character and charm. During a particularly alarming season of brush fires, a hazy red sun hung low in a darkened sky, turning the smoking canyon soaring behind the villa into a credible Vesuvius. This is, after all, the land of make-believe. An excursion to Malibu is an enchanted journey.

There is a different but equal kind of enchantment in a visit to the Getty Center. The play of the incredible California light on the tawny rough-cut travertine that changes in hue with the hour of the day; the trip up the hill by tram past flowering trees; and the arrival and discovery of buildings of a subtly layered abstraction set in a dramatic landscape that artfully rivals nature can seduce even those determined to resist its beauty. The combination of travertine walls with panels of off-white metal and the transparency of large areas of glass gives lightness and airiness to a massive undertaking. It is the locus of a great Museum conceived as a series of connecting pavilions, where one moves between treasure houses and the natural scenery for a fugue of sensuous delights.

Dedicated to excellence, the Getty Center conveys a clear image of excellence. In a democracy, excellence is supposed to be available to all. But in a curious reversal of values today, excellence has been redefined as privilege, as participation and equality denied, a perversion of meaning and application that stands excellence on its head. In this climate it is advisable to put on a populist disguise to prove that one's heart and programs are in the right place. False humility and false imagery are the frequent result, a mix of good intentions and benign hypocrisy that retreats from, rather than reinforces, democratic ideals. Davies tells us that symbolism is tacitly abandoned in an age of equality. But the messages still come through. With the Getty Trust's consolidation of all of its programs in a citadel of high art—with many of those programs directed to a different world far from this hilltop paradise—mixed messages are being sent. The Trust has chosen to build well, above anything required to serve the kind of activities that some believe have little to do with making an architectural statement. The conventional wisdom says that a choice must be made between high art and popular art, elitism and democracy, isolation or outreach, that you can't have it both ways. The Getty is caught in a clash of symbols of its own making. The truth is that this either/or formula is artificial and politically driven—these things coexist in a symbiotic relationship that serves a characteristically American crosscultural set of needs and purposes; they feed and enrich each other; they are all part of the contemporary scene. The world would be a much poorer place if no institution devoted to the public interest had ever chosen to make its position and purposes clear through the way it builds, by the generosity of its addition to the public realm. The Getty Center has the weight and presence to redistribute the balance of the fine arts from the East to the West Coast, while reinforcing Los Angeles's indigenous culture. Pride of place makes this visible and real.

There is a danger, of course; it would be tempting, when dwelling in a scholarly garden of Eden, to renounce the outside world, and there is no shortage of Cassandras who predict that this will happen. Such a course would be fatal to all of the Getty's objectives. It is essential for the public to come to the Getty, and for the Getty to remain connected to those it serves. There must be continuous two-way traffic of people and ideas up and down that hill. There is no doubt that the Museum, and the site, will be heavily visited; the Getty Center is bound to be a point of pilgrimage for schools, tourism, and the general public. All that it offers will be enjoyed without much concern about image, symbolism, or the polemics and politics of philanthropy.

That, of course, is what architecture is supposed to do—serve, support, and delight and, at its very best, awaken and elevate the sensibilities and dignify the sense of self. The direct, personal response to what one sees and feels is the final test of whether a place succeeds in human and aesthetic terms. One does not need to study questions of perception in the philosophical terms of phenomenology to know when this happens. Some are tuned in higher to their surroundings than others, with more intense responses, but we are all aware that there are places to seek out and places to avoid, that mood and well-being are affected by what we build and where we spend our time, in the most basic way.

Architectural historian and philosopher Alberto Pérez-Gómez tells us that "architecture is not an experience that words translate later." The architect Steven Holl writes that how and what we see depends on things of which we may be only partially aware—"the architectural synthesis of foreground, middle ground and distant view, together with all the subjective qualities of material and light, form the basis of 'complete perception.'" Holl describes his own reactions when he first visited the work of the great Finnish architect, Alvar Aalto. At the Säynätsalo Town Hall, "the experience of arrival was intensified by the sunny day with its play of shadow on the green grass," as he walked "from the enclosed elevated courtyard—effectively 'inside space'—into the public interior passage...." The architect is in control; he manipulates our perceptions; he leaves nothing to chance.

Something similar is experienced by the Getty visitor who leaves the tram to ascend the stone steps that lead up to the Main Plaza flanked by flowers and pine trees, lured on by the promise of the spacious entrance rotunda of the Museum beyond. With luck, the California sky is a cloudless blue and a smogless city lies at the water's sparkling edge far beneath one's feet. Groves of trees and flowering plants cascade down the hill.

Raw land has been orchestrated into a drama of all the senses by every means that art, architecture, and landscape architecture can supply. The transformation of the natural site from a high wilderness covered with wildflowers to a built environment involved a tradeoff of calculated risk. The process, to one who watched it, remains miraculous: the hill disappeared and reappeared as earth was excavated and moved; when its transient beauty proved to be unstable, the land was reinforced. Utilities were installed, roads and walls built, transportation provided, while foundations were dug and steel slowly rose. A new landscape replaced the old one. Buildings took shape as the image of the Center appeared—a place of memory and invention.

To the rest of the country, California has always been as much legend as reality, a laid-back place of dreams, tropical splendor, and eternal sun. The world has flocked to its theme parks and beaches. Now there is an alternate destination and another kind of experience, and the difference is that everything is real. If an outsider may be permitted a mildly radical thought, this could be the start of a California counter-counterculture, a return to reality from the land of make-believe. One can come to the Getty Center to see how real kings really lived, whose palaces contained the superb furnishings and boiseries now in the

Museum's period rooms. Once you start on that route nothing is faux, and reality can be a dangerously insidious thing. One becomes addicted to it, to works of art so wonderful that they take the breath away, to genuine artifacts that overwhelm with the consciousness of how the achievements of the past have survived to enrich the present. The trip from the galleries to the gardens is an enchanting transition back again to the sunlit embrace of California, with a sense of other times and places and other ways of seeing and being; this is a magic that outclasses any other kind.

A CONCERT OF WILLS   Stephen D. Rountree

This book—this project—is principally about materiality: the creation of a place, out of concrete, steel, stone, and glass, whose purpose is to celebrate, exhibit, study, preserve, and teach works of art and our collective cultural heritage. The pages that follow provide insight and, I hope, understanding into the design and construction of the unusually diverse and complex structures and spaces that make up the Getty Center. Drawings, sketches, models, and photographs will convey the material evolution of the place. But, we must also talk about people; about the vision, intellect, spirit, determination, and concerted effort of a group of men and women whose collaboration over fourteen years is, in my view, the most interesting and important element of the Getty Center story.

From the outset, we at the Getty, in our mission, have placed a strong emphasis and value upon the notion of interaction, co-action, and exchange among the several diverse programs that comprise the institution. The Getty programs are strong, relatively autonomous, and independently focused upon different aspects of the visual arts. Each entity has its own purpose, constituency, and point of view. But, the Getty, as an institution, gains meaning and impact not only from the individual efforts and contributions of the institutes, Museum, and Grant Program, but from the various ways in which each collaborates with, reflects upon, and

challenges the others, in the process affecting the way art is understood, valued, and preserved. The goal is to nurture powerful, individual voices and create a wonderful chorus.

With this as an underlying institutional objective, it is not surprising that our expectation was for both the architectural design of the Center and the process of making that architecture to achieve, simultaneously, the elegance and directness of individual expression and the power and complexity of synergy. A central problem for architect Richard Meier and the Getty team was to conceive of and design spaces and individual buildings that would respond to carefully directed, specific program needs while creating a campus that would draw these programs and their audiences together. This problem had to be resolved both functionally— the place needed to work at the level of several distinct entities as well as one large machine— and aesthetically—the architectural plan and vocabulary needed to express individuality and diversity as well as the ideals of unity, inclusivity, and synergy. Time will tell how well we achieved these goals, but in understanding the Getty Center and the process of making it, it is essential to recognize this relationship between the goals for the architecture and the mission of the Getty itself.

The work of planning, designing, and building the Center involved a similar commitment to a process of bringing together strong, independent

perspectives to bear upon a common objective. Unlike many building projects, the Getty Center started from the assumption that the client's professional staff, architect, consultants, contractor, and the community outside all were important stakeholders who, at some basic level, shared a vision. It was expected that a vigorous give-and-take among the partners—however difficult, stressful, and time-consuming—was appropriate to the complexity of the undertaking and would lead to better, richer, more responsive solutions. Getty President Harold M. Williams, Meier, and I were constantly aware of the tremendous difficulty, struggle, and effort required to orchestrate the proper balance between the several distinctive institutions that comprise the Getty and the ideal of a campus, where the architecture both signifies and enables a collaborative spirit. I am certain that there are easier ways to plan and build, but, as the following examples from the Getty Center process reveal, collaboration among empowered partners was, for us, an essential way of working.

On a project of this scale and duration, countless stories illustrate this concert of wills, but I want to focus on four: (1) the evolution of the design for the Getty Research Institute for the History of Art and the Humanities; (2) the development of the Museum's paintings galleries; (3) an unprecedented

process with the local community, leading to development rights; and (4) the unusually intense commitment of the construction team.

During 1985, the Getty management team, working closely with the Museum and institutes, developed an unusually specific and lengthy program brief for Meier and his associates. Over the course of the next two years, the ideas and concepts contained in that brief were tested as they took shape in drawings and models. Not surprisingly, our early notions were often challenged when we confronted them in three dimensions. The story of building the Research Institute is the most striking example of the design process influencing the direction of not only the building but the activity it is to contain.

In the initial program given to Meier and his associates, the nature and function of the Institute seemed clear: an advanced research institute centered around an important library, photographic archive, and special collections. While the particular scope and focus of the Institute was unique, there were existing European and American models that suggested an architectural plan for such a place. Meier's first schematic, presented in 1987, was a variation on a traditional form: a large box containing smaller boxes—one each for books, photographs, archives, visiting scholars, and staff functions— with a substantial reading room serving as the intellectual and social core. The scheme was,

of course, much more elegant than my description, and, without question, it responded to the program as it had been articulated. Nevertheless, Kurt Forster, then director of the Institute, was deeply troubled by the solution, which he saw as leading to a rigid, static configuration of the people and resources—a composition that would neither encourage nor support diverse and shifting research strategies. For Forster and his associates, this early architectural plan illuminated some fundamental issues about the nature of the institution. Instead of challenging Meier's plan, Forster's consternation led him and his staff to re-examine their own assumptions about the character of the Institute and the nature of its work. Through the deficiencies of the plan—a plan that represented well the existing organization and conception of their program—they recognized that the architecture could either be a straight jacket or a critical tool in facilitating dynamism and flexibility within the Institute. Forster pulled back for a few months and then articulated a new vision for the Institute's building that was mindful of the role of architecture and was characterized by fluidity, adaptability, and the integration of scholars, staff, and collections at almost every level. Although Meier and his associates had devoted considerable effort to the first scheme and could have been expected to resist a total reworking, they did not hesitate to take up this new charge, throwing

out the previous scheme and developing one that supported the restated objectives. Forster and Meier, along with Tom Reese, now deputy director of the Institute, spent many evenings bent over Meier's office table in Westwood, refining the plan to provide a place that would both create and respond to the dynamic qualities Forster sought to instill within the Institute. Architect and client drew from each other; the building and its purpose were almost perfectly fused. The design, as built, provides for a purposeful, fluid mixing of the resources—books, periodicals, photographs, and special collections—with visiting scholars and Getty staff. The architectural process, by bringing diverse perspectives into play, served both as a catalyst for a fresh conception of the Institute's operational strategy and as a force to enable the implementation of that strategy.

On the other side of the site, within the Museum, there was reason to worry that such a fusion might be unattainable. In the earliest days of the project, as we paced through the classic museums of Europe, it was clear that Meier and John Walsh, the Museum's director, came to the subject of gallery design and decoration with fundamentally different perspectives. For Walsh and his curators, the architectural vocabulary had to serve the primary purpose of displaying older works of art in rooms where the colors, textures, and atmosphere were completely sympathetic to the art. Walsh

was determined to have paintings galleries with the solidity, scale, proportions, light, and richness that characterized the great nineteenth-century galleries. Meier was equally convinced of the merits of his spare, modernist language. He was deeply committed to the continuity of the architectural vocabulary throughout the buildings and believed that works of art, of any period, looked best in the most austere, neutral surroundings. The tension was obvious. Yet, in the years that followed, Walsh, Meier, and their associates engaged each other in earnest, and it became clear, to me at least, that this tension would propel them both to a place neither would have found alone.

During the schematic design and early design development phases, the touchy subject of gallery decoration was avoided while the teams concentrated upon the formal qualities of the rooms and the critical issue of daylight. In response to the Museum's requirements for exhibiting paintings, Meier created solid, discrete rooms with a coved-ceiling and lantern configuration modeled after the Dulwich Gallery, and with proportions suited to older works of art. The plan was a departure from Meier's previous museum designs, yet the language of these rooms was comfortably his: the forms were elegantly simple, austere, and exacting. Walsh and his staff, mainly associate directors Deborah Gribbon and Barbara Whitney, went over the ground with Meier and

his team again and again to assure themselves that scale, proportions, and organization of the galleries—and the critical daylight element—were on the mark.

Once the rooms were right, Walsh and Meier had to face the decor. From early on, it had been clear to all involved that the period galleries for French Decorative Arts required very specialized attention and interior finishes that were far from Meier's taste and experience. New York architect Thierry Despont was retained to execute, in collaboration with the Museum's curatorial and conservation staff, the interior design of those galleries, working with the Meier office to fit the seventeenth- and eighteenth-century rooms into the overall plan. For the paintings galleries, however, the Museum was insistent upon colors, finishes, and ornaments that would complement the paintings and sculpture, while Meier urged restraint, advocating a much more neutral, subtler palette that would correspond to the building's modernist complexion. Meier was unable to generate much personal enthusiasm for oak wainscoting and colored fabric wall coverings. It was decided that a facilitator and intermediary was needed, and Thierry Despont, who had earned everyone's respect, was asked to take up the challenge.

Despont worked with Meier, often in New York, to build a greater level of comfort with the colors and textures so critical to the sympathetic display of older European paintings and to draw his talents into a constructive review of options. At the same time, he worked with Walsh and the curatorial staff to arrive at simpler details and a subtler use of textures while maintaining the use of rich colors and deep-toned wood. Despont, working with Deborah Gribbon in particular, brought a rationality and organization to the decor that appealed to Meier. With numerous mockups and review sessions, the give-and-take eventually produced the paintings galleries we see today: rooms that are decidedly contemporary in their essential architectural qualities, which show Meier's strong hand, yet that embrace the older works of art with traditional proportions, wood elements, rich colors, and textured surfaces, all with lively daylight from above. Walsh, Meier, Despont, Gribbon, and dozens of others brought strong, disparate points of view to bear upon a shared objective, and both the art and the architecture have been well served by their struggle.

This sort of intense, painstaking effort was repeated in nearly every corner of the Getty Center, as we insisted upon a design process that took full account of very particular needs while, at the same time, attending to the broader objectives of making a coherent and integrated architecture for the campus as a whole. The dialogue took time. Within the Getty we were not always, or even usually, pleased to listen to arguments for architectural nuance over our well-considered and exacting program requirements. Yet, Meier and his associates were unrelenting in forcing us to confront desires that undermined the integrity of the architecture. Those of us managing the process simply insisted upon a patient, if painful, airing and examination of options. We could not allow ourselves the luxury of taking the easy way and thereby settling for solutions that sacrificed either program or architecture, or both. Meier and/or his partner Michael Palladino and I had countless, exhausting sessions, in which we tugged and pulled at each other over such matters. While we were often coming at the issues from different vantage points, we shared a commitment to find the best possible resolution, constantly worrying that we might overlook something. In the end, seemingly distinct components of the campus have, I believe, been pulled together by a strong, consistent formal vocabulary, a unity in the materials, and a subtle composition of elements referencing and playing off of each other. While we at the Getty all started with a fundamental belief in the capacity of architecture to transform experience, I do not think any of us could have foreseen the difficulty in opening up to the architect so that the buildings might actually achieve that power.

Over the course of the Getty Center project, a good deal was written about the long, difficult process of negotiation and conciliation among the Getty, the community surrounding the site, and city officials. Most often, this process was portrayed as a matter of absolute contention and conflict. However, that view is terribly simplistic and denies, to those involved, the fact that the parties appreciated both the importance of the Getty Center for the city and the legitimacy of community concerns over its potential negative impacts. In a collaborative way—not unlike dealing with the design of the galleries or the character of the Research Institute—we had to find a way for the architecture and site plan to respond to the needs and fears of our neighbors and to the city's requirements while still meeting the overriding objective of serving a broad public audience and our diverse professional constituencies.

As with all other aspects of the project, this problem could only be solved by those determined to make it happen—individual neighbors, city officials, Meier and his associates, and several representatives from the Getty. Over the years, a small and remarkably consistent group of people met and spoke together on more than 150 occasions, addressing such issues as building mass, building height, lighting, noise, privacy, lines of sight, traffic, drainage, and landscape. Issues ranged from something as fundamental as the height of the structures housing Museum galleries

to an item as specific as the placement of two or three trees to screen a view into a neighboring yard. Unlike most commercial projects, we at the Getty saw ourselves as a permanent fixture in the neighborhood with a vested interest in long-term relationships. Thus, we were determined to work at the issues patiently and painstakingly in order to avoid rash compromises on our part and to create an honest, ongoing dialogue. Meier and I spent many evenings in local neighbors' living rooms, or at a neighborhood synagogue, talking through the concerns and attempting to devise solutions. Our neighbors devoted a great deal of their time and came to understand both our operating objectives and Meier's architectural concerns. Certainly there were difficult, contentious issues, but we all kept returning to table, intent upon finding answers. The result was many relatively small accommodations, made over several years, of the design and construction process, aimed at containing the visual and environmental impact of the Getty Center—accommodations that were significant from our neighbors' perspective but that did not compromise either the architecture or programs.

Of course, the Getty Center is not only about design, it is about building, and the construction process itself mirrored the values, attitudes, and struggles I have described above. It was always clear to us and to Dinwiddie Construction Company, the general contractor, that this project would be very unusual in terms of its scale, its purposes, the quality of the workmanship, the complexity of the structures, the prominent site, and the project's high profile in the media. Still, I had imagined that this was basically a management perspective and that it would be difficult, if not impossible, to communicate the meaning and importance of the project to the hundreds of men and women working for the many construction firms on the project. However, the construction workers were among the first to fully appreciate the project's unique qualities and they took great pride and ownership of it.

An example of participation from the field was the effort of the contractor, DBM/Hatch, Inc., in installing the stone. The architect's vision for the cladding of the buildings called for the regular and precise alignment of the stone. The challenge for the contractor was applying these specifications throughout the many varied conditions of the building complex. To accomplish this, Hatch created and installed over 150 different types of "clips" necessary to set the stone, enabling workers to meet Meier's aesthetic.

The Dinwiddie management and the Getty's Curt Williams understood that the workers had to feel a strong sense of direct responsibility if we were to achieve the sort of quality we were seeking. This partnership was nurtured by Meier himself, who frequently wandered the site and engaged directly with workers and supervisors over details that caught his attention. While his words were as often critical as laudatory, the people on the job appreciated Meier's regular, direct involvement and realized that what they were doing mattered; each person made a difference.

Without question, the project's long duration and demanding nature gave many of us the opportunity to develop relationships over the course of years, not months. Elevator operators, carpenters, iron workers, stone masons, plasterers, area supervisors, traffic controllers—all became old friends to those of us who were frequently on the site. This feeling of community was a source of reassurance and strength when we were facing tough field problems or pushing the schedule to the limit.

There were, of course, tensions between those who designed the Center, those who built it, and those who would pay for it and use it. I suppose that each of us, in our own way, perceived the stakes as being somewhat greater than typical, and the problems as being unusually complicated and difficult. In some measure, the deep sense of

personal pride and ownership that developed on all sides raised the temperature of passionate advocacy and argument; the Getty Center was an all-consuming occupation for many of us. But, as with other aspects of the design and planning process, there was a clear understanding that this was an undertaking of partners, that we needed each other, and that passion, commitment, and discourse, however stressed, were necessary to get to the right result. Almost every square inch of the nearly two million square feet was scrutinized, evaluated, tested, debated, and, often, contested. We all believed that each decision mattered, and each of us knew that the others cared just as much as we ourselves did.

The Getty Center will now take its place in the fabric of Los Angeles's public life. Whatever else the people of the Getty organization produce in the coming century, it is clear that this place is already recognized as an important fixture in the region, a refreshing and inspiring place to be, a symbol of confidence in the future and reverence for the past. The place itself, like the art it celebrates and explores, is the product not of machines, but of human inspiration and effort. For each of us involved in making this place, the undertaking has been an extraordinary and wonderful privilege.

A VISION FOR PERMANENCE

Richard Meier

The Getty Center takes its form from the opportunities and constraints of a magnificent hilltop site. Located just off the San Diego Freeway in the foothills of the Santa Monica Mountains, the site is immediately accessible to the flow of urban life and yet slightly removed from the city. The hilltop offers panoramic views of the ocean and mountains, but it also overlooks the geometry of Los Angeles, which is spread like a vast, elegant carpet below the rugged terrain.

In choosing how to organize the buildings, landscaping, and open spaces, I deferred to the site's topography. There are two natural ridges— one lines up with the street grid of Los Angeles and the second with the swing of the San Diego Freeway as it turns north through the Sepulveda Pass. The buildings form axes along these two ridges. During the design process, we were concerned with relating the program to the site, creating ideal conditions in which to display, view, conserve, and study art. We were also concerned with the way the Getty Center is experienced, both on site and from afar. So, we located the more public programs—the Museum, Conservation Institute, Education Institute, Information Institute, Grant and Administration offices, and the Auditorium—along the eastern ridge, where they rise boldly from the crest of the hill and present a clear, public face for the Getty. The residential neighborhoods adjacent to the western

ridge face the more modest profile of the Research Institute for the History of Art and the Humanities, which houses, among other activities, the Center's more inwardly focused program of scholarly pursuits.

Just as one can best appreciate the layout of Rome from its elevated landmarks, so does the hilltop site of the Getty Center offer the best place to see and understand Los Angeles. To make the most of this opportunity, the architecture frames small vignettes and expansive panoramas. It heightens awareness of nature and the city, from downtown to the mountains and ocean—on a clear day, even to Catalina Island. A place apart, yet firmly connected to the world beyond, the Getty Center is visible, accessible, and open to all.

I liken the formal organization of the Getty to a university campus, but some have compared it to the Acropolis because of its prominence, sense of permanence, and the way the buildings relate to each other on a hilltop setting. It is thirty years since I last visited the Acropolis in Athens, but who could not be inspired by some of the ideas— of procession, circulation, and movement—that are expressed there? Another analogy that has been made in terms of formal relationships is Hadrian's Villa at Tivoli. Clearly there is no physical resemblance in the architecture, but again it is in

the formal concepts—here of asymmetry and surprise, and of the long walls that extend into the landscape relating built form to nature. Another, more modern tradition—that of the Southern California houses of Rudolf Schindler, Richard Neutra, and Frank Lloyd Wright—can be recalled in the Center's sense of openness and crisp horizontality.

The Getty Trust, led by its visionary president, Harold M. Williams, bought the site before anyone knew exactly how much legally could be built there, and the process required long and patient negotiations with the city authorities and the neighborhood homeowners' associations to fit all the programmatic elements within the zoning envelope. Working closely with Stephen D. Rountree, the thoughtful and sensitive building program director, my task was to turn the agreed limitations to best advantage. Wanting to maintain as much open space as possible, rather than cover the hilltop with buildings, the solution to me was to excavate.

Working with the imposed height limitations of 45 feet on the west side of the site and 65 feet on a portion of the east, more than half of the space of the Getty Center has been placed below ground level. Most of the buildings are three stories above ground and three below; all are linked at a common level by subterranean corridors that are used for functions such as moving books and bringing in supplies. All below-grade offices receive natural light from sunken gardens or from windows set into the perimeter slopes. Artificially lit spaces with no natural light, such as corridors, mechanical and electrical rooms, storage areas, reserve book stacks, and laboratories, are brightened with color to give each a distinctive character.

This was my first commission in California, and like so many easterners and Europeans before me, I was dazzled by the clarity of light and the extraordinary climate in Los Angeles. To build here as one might elsewhere is to squander a great opportunity. Two years after starting work on the Getty, I completed an oceanfront house in Malibu. That project gave me an opportunity to experiment, on a small scale, with the mingling of interior and exterior spaces, and with the movement of people through a succession of indoor and outdoor rooms. At the Getty, galleries, offices, and the Auditorium all lead out into courtyards and terraces, and the alternation of ceiling and sky is a crucial element of the design. I had even hoped to have one level of the Cafe left unwalled, but realized that even in beautiful Southern California it could sometimes be too wet or windy for outdoor eating year round.

The Getty Center hosts multiple programs. A single building, serving as many as three different entities of the Getty Trust, needed to be tailored to the specific needs and preferences of them all. While satisfying the program of each institution, I wanted to make the Center a harmonious whole. For this reason, the spaces between the buildings became crucial to the design, because they belong to everyone. They are part of the fabric of the Center, holding things together, establishing a sense of intimacy and human scale. There is a sense of progression from the tram to the Arrival Plaza, up the great staircase and ramp to the Museum, and around the buildings to lookout points that anchor the axes of the Center.

In collaboration with landscape architects Dan Kiley, Laurie Olin, and Emmet Wemple, we developed a plan for the landscape that is, in some ways, as important as the buildings themselves. In time, when the plantings assert themselves, they will help define the spaces between the buildings. For example, the wisteria covering the trellis beside the Restaurant, in conjunction with mature trees, will form a screen around the Arrival Plaza. There is a balance between natural and man-made, and the hardscaped Arrival Plaza will be put to good use for formal and informal gatherings, and for outdoor performances in which the steps leading up to the Museum are used for seating.

When I compare early sketches and design models with what has been built, it is remarkable how the original conceptual ideas have remained intact—particularly since every piece of the complex was discussed, scrutinized, redesigned, reworked, and repriced. Since the Getty is a new, developing institution, there were many changes and refinements in programs and needs as we were designing. Every decision, down to the color of a wall, was made by a group rather than an individual, and many decisions were driven by budgetary concerns. This is an expensive building, but not unreasonably so, and sacrifices had to be made. A bridge linking the Auditorium and Trust offices was eliminated; the retaining wall along the service road was faced with stucco, not stone. I regret these and many other changes, but some improved the design. For example, at one point we were over budget and nobody wanted to give up a single space. So we reduced the size of the buildings project by 12 percent. The result was a compression of the plan that pulled things more tightly together and reduced costs.

The impact of the seismic code, and the Getty's understandable desire to go far beyond the customary requirements following the 1994 earthquake, made its demands on the architecture as well. The exposed structural columns had to be made much thicker than originally intended, and in some places this distorts the vertical/horizontal relationship.

From the beginning, I had thought of stone as a way of grounding the buildings and giving them a sense of permanence. Stone has been used for retaining walls and the bases of all the buildings, and repetitive metal—a lighter, more fluid, less expensive material for cladding—have been utilized for the upper stories and curvilinear elements. This division in the use of materials accommodates the shifts of height across the site, creating a baseline at the Museum entrance level with stone below and metal panels predominating above. Both cladding elements conform to a 2-foot, 6-inch module, a scaling device that is keyed to ceiling heights and floor dimensions.

We undertook an extensive worldwide search for the right stone. Some proved too expensive, others came from quarries too small to produce the quantity of material we needed. Someone suggested travertine, but today it is commonly used as a veneer and I wanted something that would offer the substance and surface texture of traditional masonry. I had seen rough-cut, richly textured samples of limestone, which were too soft and too expensive for our purposes, so we sought to achieve a similar effect with travertine.

Turning to Italy, where ancient and classical Rome was largely built of travertine, we worked with the family-owned Mariotti quarries in Bagni di Tivoli. Over a year, we developed a technique of using a guillotine to split blocks of travertine along fault lines. After many tries, we were able to achieve the 2-foot, 6-inch squares that we needed. It was also the largest size piece that could be cut without crushing the stone with the falling blade.

Splitting stone this way is very efficient. Rough-surfaced pieces six inches thick are generated, then two inches on either side are sawed off for exterior wall panels, and the smooth-sided middle cut is used as pavers. Nothing is wasted. Going through the quarries, I found large rough stones that were particularly beautiful and said to Carlo Mariotti and his sons, "Don't cut these; we'll work them into a wall somewhere." About a dozen of these stones are incorporated into the regular grid for a change of scale and color, to break things up, and mark a key point. The masons have taken pride in selecting stones with exposed fossils and installing them at eye level, where their textures enrich the building's surface. I also found several large blocks that had been lying in water at the quarry for many years and had them cut in two and used as benches.

The design of the travertine exterior wall is based upon an open-joint panel system, which we have developed in our European work, in contrast to the American technique of sealing the joints with mortar. By allowing water to drain behind the outer skin, the European method protects the surface from streaking and ensures that the buildings will look as good tomorrow as they do today. Throughout the complex, the irregular profile of the blocks catches the light in an extraordinary way, changing color throughout the day.

To complement the colors and texture of the stone, an off-white color was selected for the metal panels. The choice of color was negotiated with the homeowners' associations, selected from among fifty minutely varied shades. Pure white has been used only for the Center's tram shelter, the drum of the Museum, the courtyard of the Research Institute, and in smaller details such as handrails, highlighting, or giving hierarchy to specific components of the building composition.

Visitors to the Getty Center will ride the tram from the parking garage at the base of the hill to the Arrival Plaza at the top. Both for the sake of convenience and to maintain the unencumbered beauty of the site, we located the main parking garage at the bottom, immediately off the freeway. But not everyone can be expected to walk to the top, and shuttle buses would have been noisy and intrusive. The solution was to build a tram— a kind of automatic, horizontal elevator. Visitors await the tram beneath an open-sided canopy that frames the Center on the skyline. On the way up, the tram hugs a line of trees; the site unfolds as

The travertine originates from Bagni di Tivoli, where stone deposits three hundred feet thick have been quarried for over two thousand years. An automated guillotine system developed for the Getty Center project split blocks of travertine, producing two pieces with the rough cleft surface. Nearly three hundred thousand pieces of travertine were installed as either building cladding or paving.

the visitor ascends, offering changing views of the freeway and cityscape below.

From the Arrival Plaza, a broad flight of steps leads up to the Museum, which is the largest and most publicly visited part of the Center. As such, it occupies the southeast corner of the hilltop, where it overlooks the city. At the entrance to the Museum, the visitor can look through a glass-walled lobby into a garden court, where little jets of water spill into a long, rock-filled pool shaded by a row of trees.

When I first visited the Getty Museum in Malibu, I marveled at the ease with which one passes from gallery to garden court and back again. I found that freedom unique, unlike any museum I had ever visited. It was something that I wanted to bring to the new hilltop site. John Walsh, the Museum's director, who had devoted much time and thought to formulating the Museum's program and articulating the ambience and philosophy of the museum experience, did not want any prescribed paths for visiting the Museum. He wanted freedom of choice, with routes that were fluid and criss-crossing. Hence, one can explore the galleries in sequence or at random, at first- or second-story level, without having to retrace one's steps. In the interplay of interior and exterior space, one always knows where one is and where one has been, without fear of getting lost.

By integrating the gardens with the architecture, and by providing visitors access to the extraordinary views on all sides, I sought to intensify the experience of viewing art while at the same time helping to avert fatigue. One looks at art but also enjoys opportunities to look away, to rest and think, before moving on. This combination of concentration with relaxation makes museum-going less confining and exhausting.

There are two types of galleries. Those on the upper level, housing paintings and sculpture, have skylights with overhead louvers that filter the natural light and adjust it according to the time of day and the changing weather. These top-lit galleries open into glass-walled corridors. The galleries on the lower level are, for the most part, artificially lit, since they require lower-light levels for the displays of works on paper and decorative arts. Small, medium, and large rooms are arranged around interior or exterior courtyards, giving each cluster of galleries a sense of place. One could think of the building as a single museum or as a series of pavilions.

Although the Museum will be the principal destination for most of the public, it is not the only attraction at the Getty Center. Visitors can attend lectures, colloquia, concerts, and films in the steeply raked 450-seat Auditorium. They can have a meal

in the Restaurant or the Cafe across the plaza, enjoying spectacular views of the ocean. And they can explore the landscaping that covers most of the hill.

A more private part of the Center, the Research Institute, is located on the southwest part of the hilltop, overlooking the site's residential side and the ocean. This location was selected to accommodate the Institute's function as a building used primarily by visiting scholars and staff, with limited access for students and professionals. For the public, there is also a small exhibition space located near the entrance. The Institute's former director, Kurt Forster, invented a new program for a kind of institution that never before existed, which evolved as the design of the building evolved. He and I worked very closely in planning the design, whose curved form evokes the introspective nature of scholarly research and whose translucence promotes the exchange of ideas.

The materials of scholarship—reference works, book stacks, and reading areas—are integrated with one another and wrapped in a spiral around a central courtyard. A ramp creates concentric circulation paths, linking the activities of this open plan and promoting interaction among the scholars. A mix of offices, study carrels, and seminar rooms—designed later with the Institute's director, Salvatore Settis—opens onto terraces, courtyards, and open stack areas, all of which have a variety of relationships both to books and to outside garden spaces. The Institute looks inward and outward at the same time; it is separate but related to the larger whole of the Getty Center.

Two buildings are located to the north and east of the Arrival Plaza: one houses the offices of the Getty Trust and Information Institute; the other contains the Conservation Institute, the Education Institute, and the Grant Program. As in the rest of the Getty Center, these two buildings relate to the landscape, their intimate gardens and outdoor terraces providing for fluid movement between interior and exterior spaces. The facades integrate exterior sunscreens, which makes it possible to control the level of sunlight without closing the interior shades.

Each building has its own reception lobby, helping to provide an identity for the separate programs housed within. These identities are reinforced through a variety of interior plans and expressions. For example, the Conservation Institute uses an entirely open plan, without enclosed offices, while the Trust utilizes a more traditional mix of open plan and private offices. Working with each of the program directors—Miguel Angel Corzo, Lani Lattin Duke, Eleanor Fink, and Deborah Marrow—we designed the building envelopes and interiors to suit the programs' individual needs and desires for working space.

The Getty is an institution of many parts. Until now, these have been scattered throughout the city and little understood. The Getty Center has been built to draw them together, serving the different constituents on a single site. Yet the Center is more than an enclave or a campus. Its setting is idyllic, yet it is related to the real world, which is visible and present all around. Many will come to the Getty Center on impulse—to stroll through the Museum, have a meal, or visit the gardens—and find their lives enriched. The Center can serve as an oasis for mind and body, a valuable addition to the public realm in an increasingly privatized and fragmented city.

Many are likely to come to the Getty Center just for the views. From the hilltop terraces and gardens, one can see and understand the physical form of Los Angeles more clearly than from any other location. The architecture frames small vignettes and expansive panoramas, and it intensifies one's perception of changing light and color. It gives visitors a heightened awareness of nature and the city: the flats, foothills, and distant mountains, the Pacific Ocean, and, on a clear day, the island of Catalina. A place apart, yet firmly connected to the world beyond, the Center is visible, accessible, and open to all.

Richard Meier

SITE DIAGRAMS, MODELS, AND PLANS

Context and Geometry
The site has two natural ridges: one lines up with the street grid of
Los Angeles and the second, with the swing of the San Diego Freeway
as it turns north through the Sepulveda Pass. The master plan for the
project responds to this natural topography and the site's orientation
within the urban fabric of Los Angeles.

Landscape

A landscape pattern of over 3,000 native oaks covers the portion of the building site that is undeveloped, mediating between the natural chapparal and the built environment.

Exterior Spaces

The exterior public spaces derive their placement and proportion from the project axes and building masses.

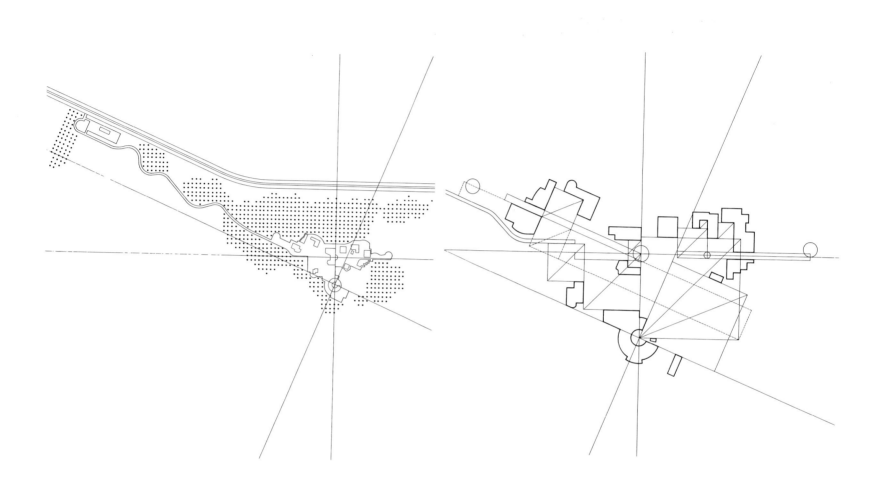

Structure

The architectural massing hierarchy is articulated through the structural system. Stone walls (indicated in bold) interplay with a structural system that separates walls from supports, allowing lighter, more transparent walls.

Circulation

Within the Museum, circulation is linked among the pavilions; within the other buildings, the circulation is self-contained.

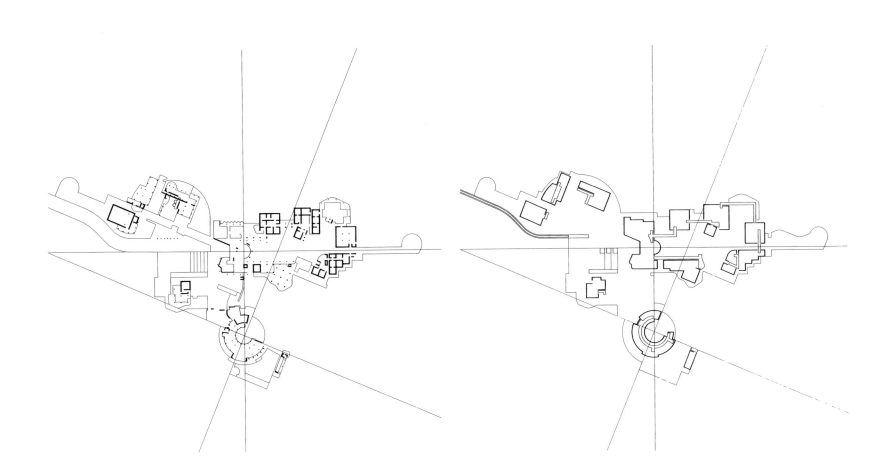

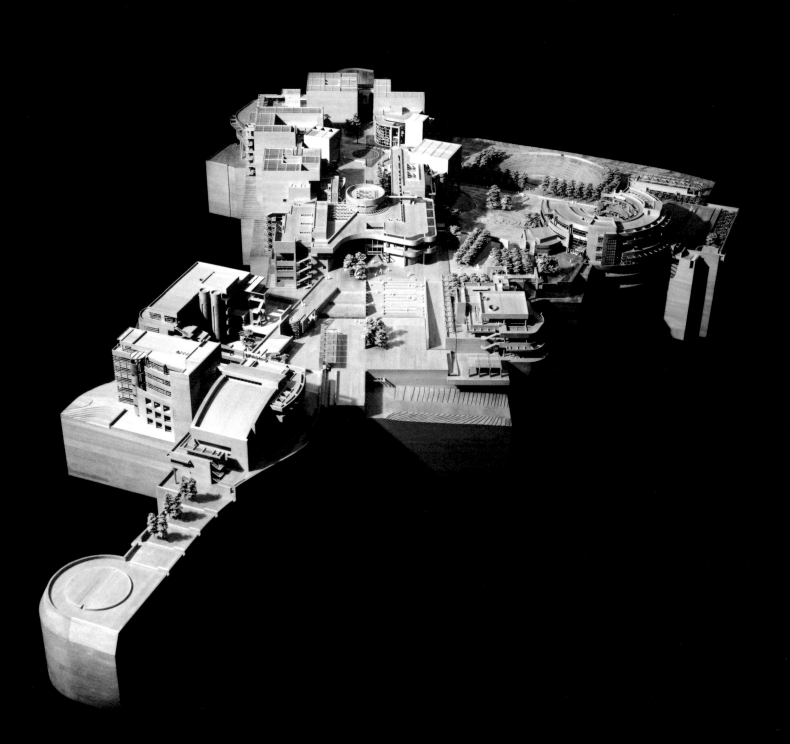

Final Model, 1993
View to south

Final Model, 1993
View to west

North Elevation

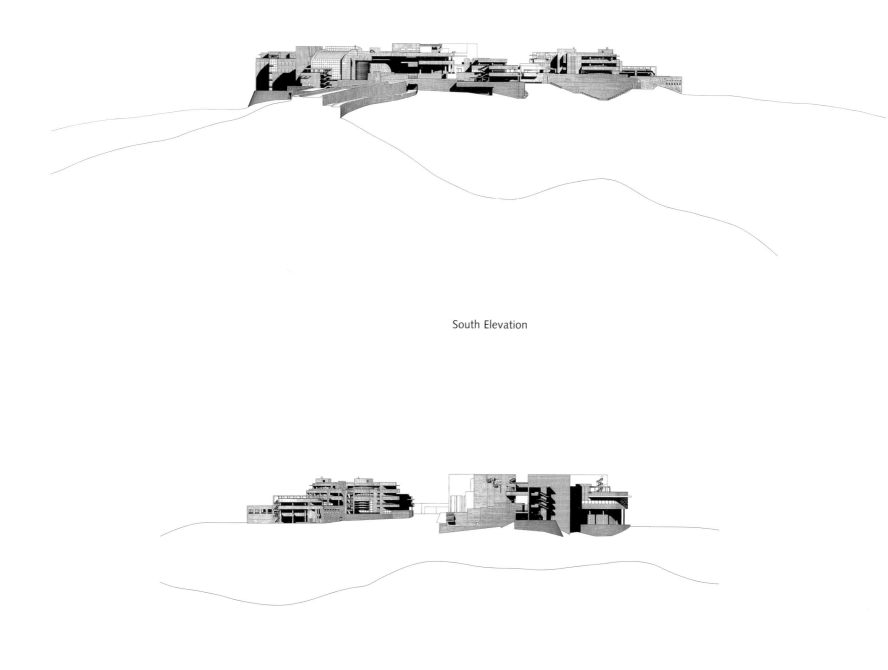

South Elevation

West Elevation

East Elevation

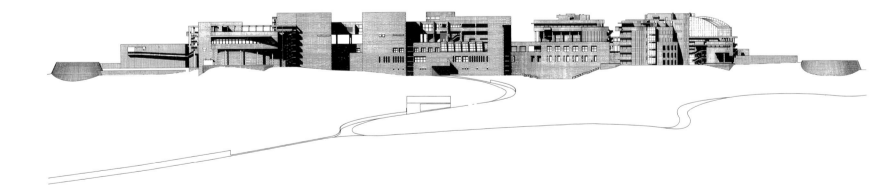

Key Plan

North Building:
The Getty Information Institute
The J. Paul Getty Trust

East Building:
The Getty Conservation Institute
The Getty Education Institute for the Arts
The Getty Grant Program

Auditorium

The J. Paul Getty Museum

Tram Station

Central Garden

Restaurant and Cafe

The Getty Research Institute for the
History of Art and the Humanities

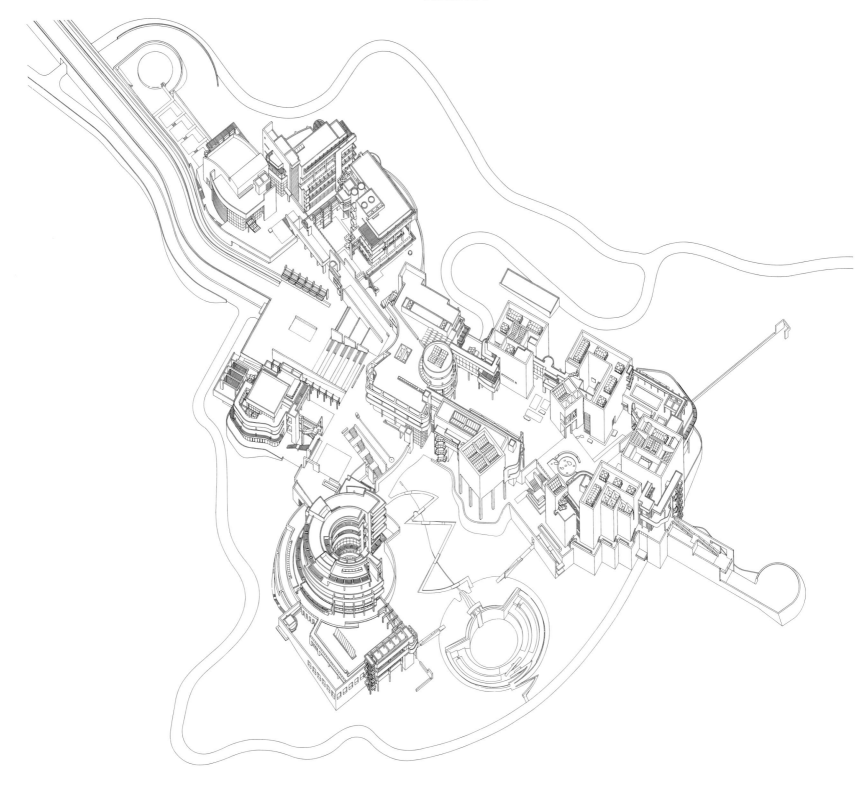

Final Site Plan with Landscape

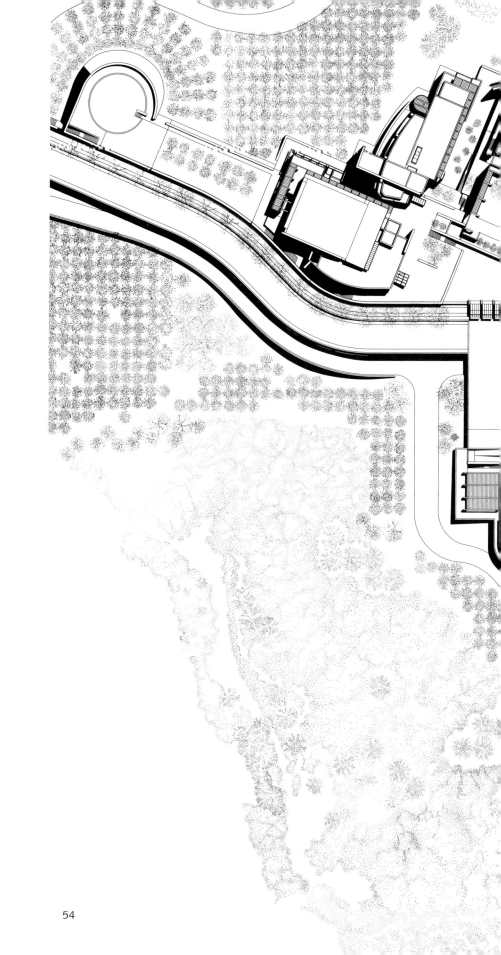

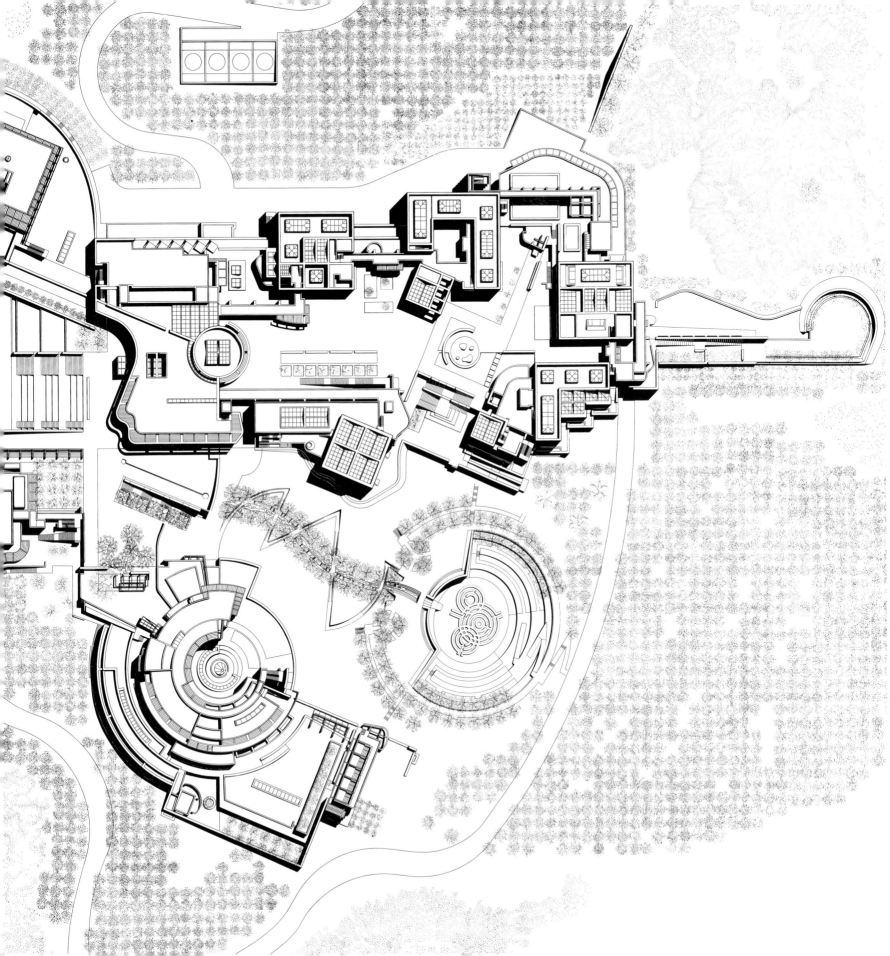

Site Plan
Plaza level

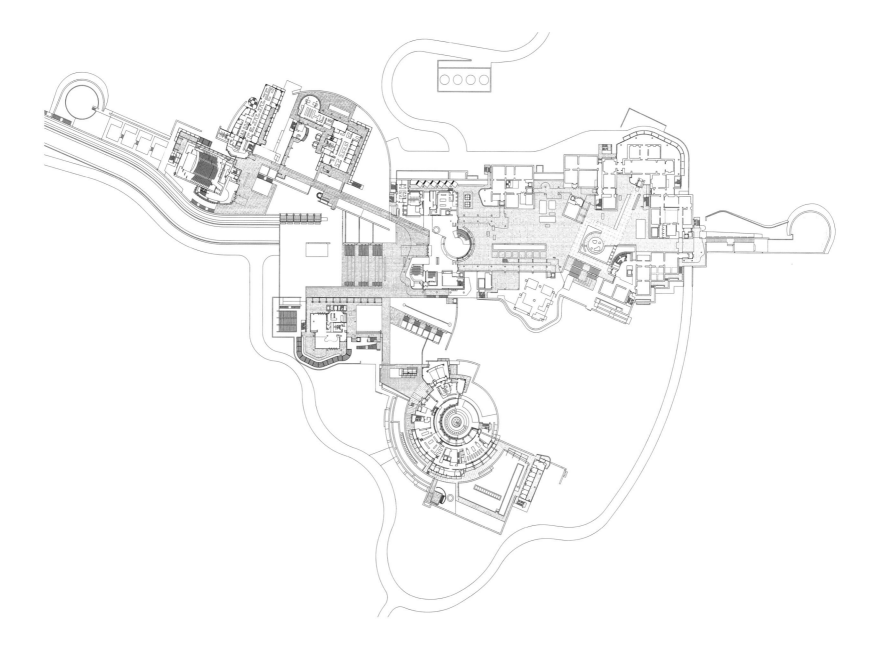

Site Plan
Second level

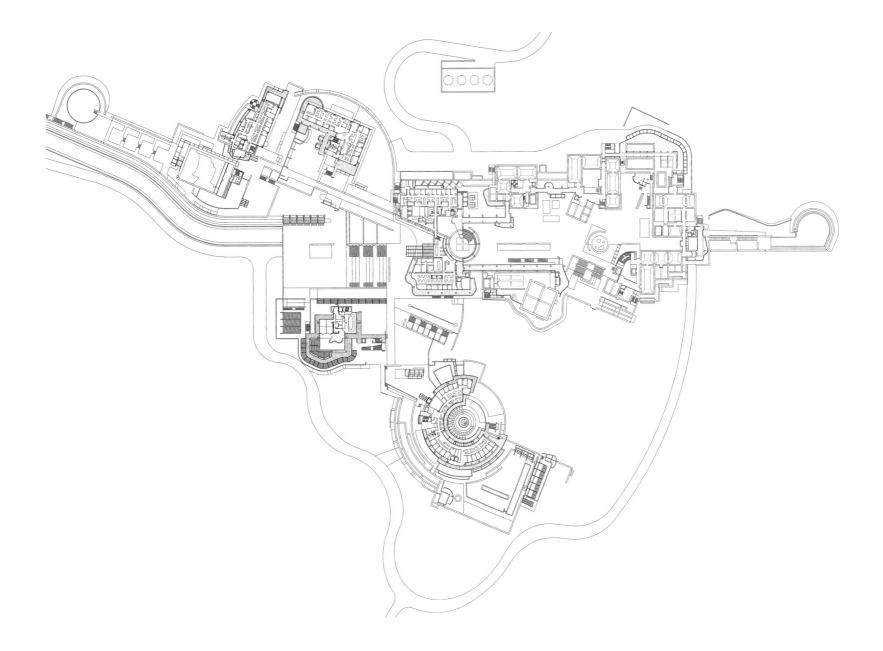

Auditorium, North Building, East Building, Restaurant/Cafe
Plaza level

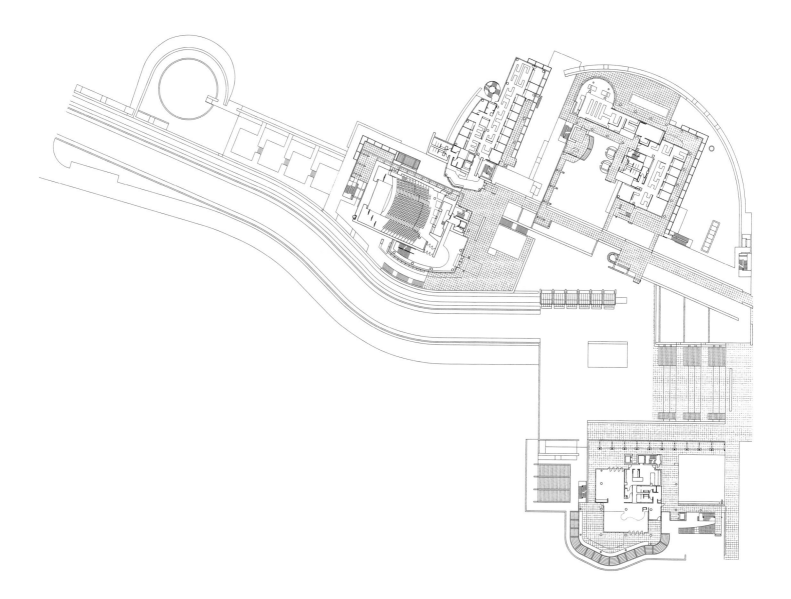

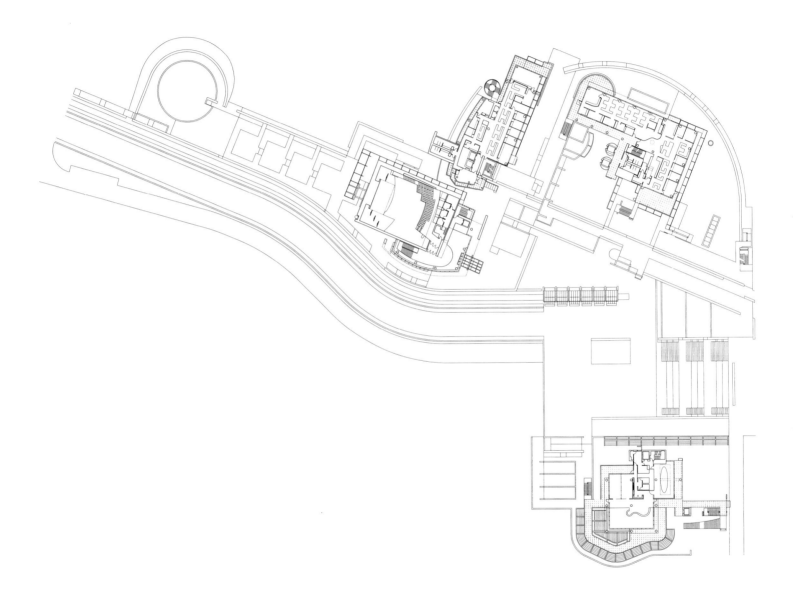

Research Institute
Third lower level

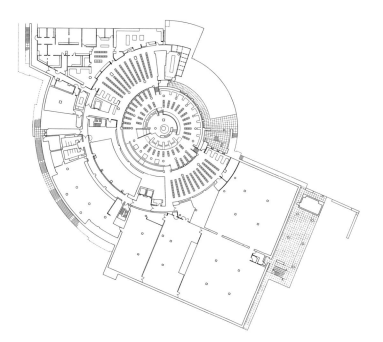

Research Institute
Second lower level

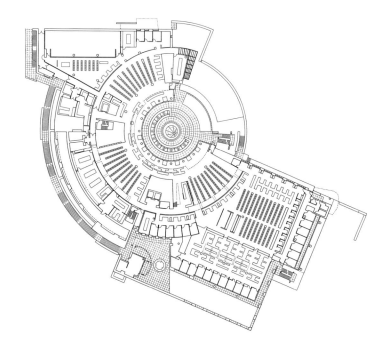

Research Institute
Plaza level

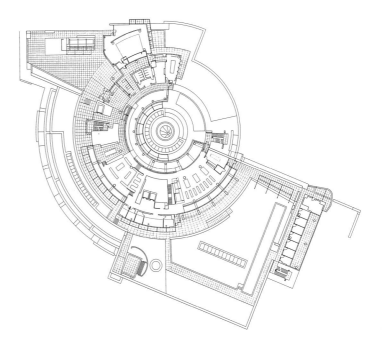

Research Institute
Second level

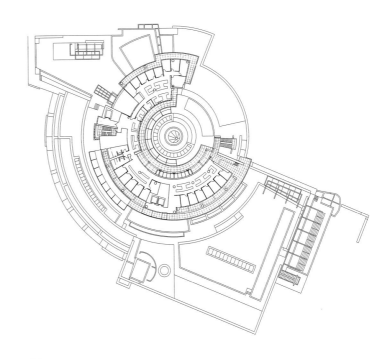

Museum
Plaza level

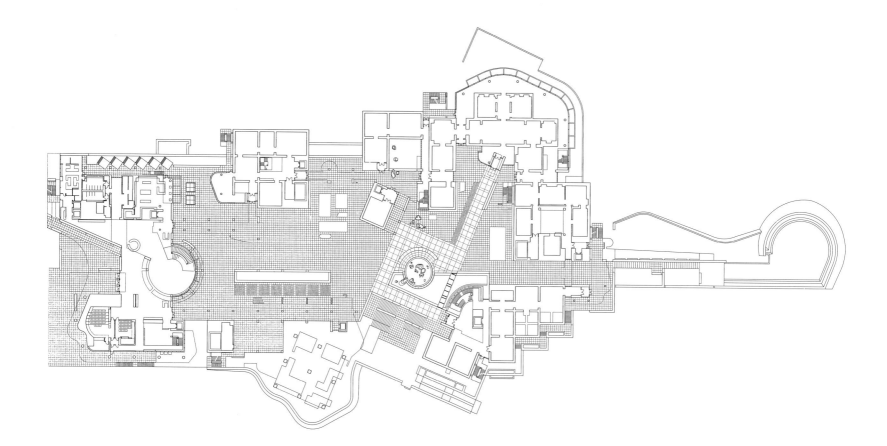

Museum
Second level

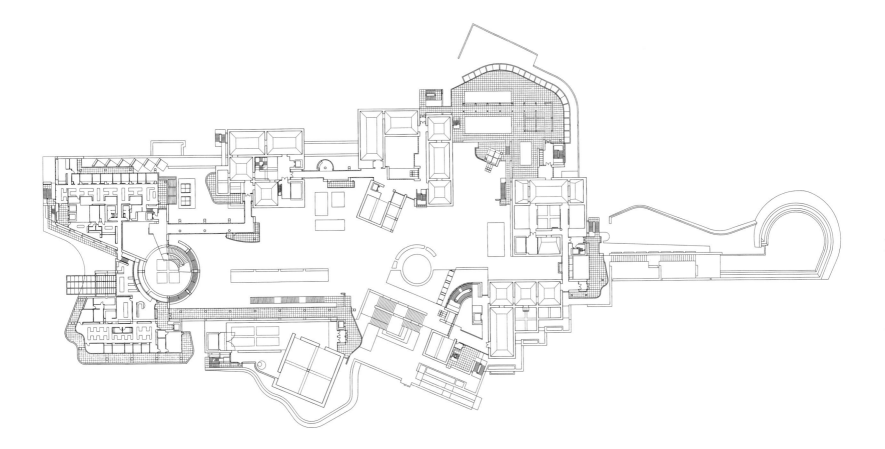

THE MUSEUM'S DECORATIVE ARTS GALLERIES

The Museum's program called for a series of galleries in which to present its large, and significant, collection of seventeenth-, eighteenth-, and early nineteenthth-century Decorative Arts. In 1989, New York architect Thierry Despont was hired to design these galleries with Museum curator Gillian Wilson. Despont's challenge was to create galleries appropriate to the Museum's Decorative Arts collection while fitting these galleries into the building plan developed by Richard Meier & Partners. The result of this collaboration is a sequence of galleries of varying scale and ornament. In some cases, the galleries are designed to evoke, but not imitate, rooms from the corresponding historical period through the use of floor patterns, fabrics, wall finishes, and architectural details such as moldings. Other galleries have actual eighteenthth-century wall paneling and are reconstructions of the original rooms themselves. Designing and installing the Decorative Arts galleries required an especially complex process of sensitive design, scholarly and technical research, and expert workmanship. As part of his design process, Despont created a series of pen-and-ink studies and watercolor elevations for each of the rooms, a selection of which appears on the following pages.

Floor Plan
Museum
Decorative Arts galleries

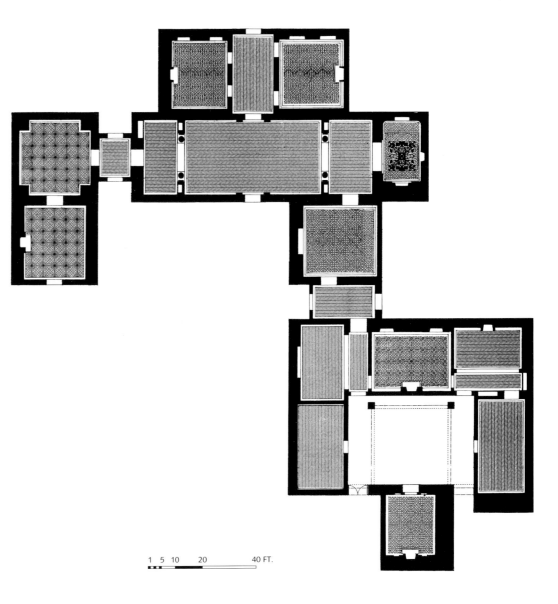

1 5 10   20   40 FT.

Preliminary Sketches
1986–1988

Presentation Drawings

French Decorative Arts
1750–1760

French Furniture
1660–1710

Neoclassical Paneled Room

French Tapestries

CONSTRUCTION
View to north
December, 1992

July, 1994

October, 1995

February, 1997

View to south
May, 1992

September, 1994

September, 1995

December, 1996

View to east
December, 1992

July, 1995

April, 1996

January, 1997

View to west
May, 1992

October, 1993

June, 1995

February, 1997

In early 1984, the Getty Trust commissioned
Joe Deal to create a photographic documentation
of the building of the Getty Center. The resulting
photographs not only objectively record the
construction of the site and the building, but also
subjectively interpret the transformed landscape.
Over thirteen years, Deal produced a portfolio
of more than 150 photographs, a selection
of which follows.

79

Bruce Bourassa worked on the Getty Center
as a construction foreman from 1995 through the
spring of 1997. During this time, he created
a portfolio of portraits of those who contributed
to the making of the Getty Center. A group
of these photographs are presented in the pages
that follow.

Museum
South Promontory
View to east

THE GETTY CENTER
Spring, 1997

Auditorium *(left)*, Restaurant/Cafe *(right)*,
View to south

North Promontory *(left foreground)*,
Auditorium *(right)*, North Building *(left)*
View to south

Auditorium
View to north

Auditorium
Lower level stairs leading to Arrival Plaza
View to south

Auditorium
Entrance
View to west

Auditorium
Entrance
View to north

Auditorium
Lobby
View to west

Auditorium
Interior

East Plaza Walkway
View to west from East Building entrance

North Building
Lobby
View to north

North Building
Exterior stairs
View to north

North Building
East Terrace
View to south

East Building
View to north from Museum Terrace

Corridor to North Building
Second lower level
View to north

Palm Garden
East Building *(left)*
North Building *(right)*
View to west

East Building
Second lower level
View to north

East Building
Interiors

East Building (*foreground*) and Museum (*background*)
View to south

East Building
East Terrace
View to north

OVERLEAF:
East Building
Conservation Institute
Information Center
View to north

Arrival Plaza
Elevator
View to south

Arrival Plaza
View to north

PREVIOUS PAGE:
Arrival Plaza *(foreground)*
Auditorium, North Building, East Building *(left to right)*
View to east

OVERLEAF:
Stairs leading to Main Plaza *(foreground)*
Auditorium, East Building, North Building *(left to right)*
View to north

Restaurant/Cafe
View to west

Cafe
North Terrace
View to south

Cafe
West Terrace
View to north

Restaurant
Interior

Cafe
Interior

Research Institute
Interior
Third lower level

Research Institute
View to west from
Restaurant Terrace

Museum
Entrance

Stairs leading
to Main Plaza
and Museum Entrance
from Arrival Plaza

Museum
Lobby

Museum
West Pavilion lobby
Stair detail

Museum
West Pavilion lobby

Museum
Courtyard and lobby
View to north from West Pavilion

Museum
Interior passageway between North and East Pavilions

Museum
Interior passageway of East Pavilion

Museum
North Pavilion lobby

EXIT

EXIT

Museum
South Pavilion atrium
View to Neoclassical Paneled Room

Museum
View through Decorative Arts galleries

Museum
View through galleries
before installation

Museum
Skylight in
South Pavilion atrium

OVERLEAF:
Main Plaza
View to north from Museum Entrance

CENTRAL GARDEN

From the earliest vision and planning stages for the Getty Center, we intended that the gardens would play an integral role in the experience of the Center. In 1992, as we reviewed Richard Meier's preliminary concept for the Central Garden area, we concluded that we wanted to introduce an overtly aesthetic dimension to the garden, to have it function as a work of art and not only as a setting for the architecture. We also recognized that this garden would be one opportunity to incorporate an additional voice into the conception of the Getty Center. Our sense was that countervailing aesthetics would enliven and challenge one another, making the visitor's experience richer and more meaningful overall. This interest in diverse perspectives was, after all, one of the underlying principles in establishing the various, and distinct, programs of the Getty and will continue to inform our activities.

The desire to further broaden and enrich the visitor's experience led to our inviting artist Robert Irwin to create a site-contextual piece for the Central Garden. Over the next year, Irwin and Meier worked together to identify where Irwin's piece would best fit in to the complex. Irwin's plan for the garden—the evolution of which is presented in the following pages—sprung from his response to the context of the powerful, controlled geometries of the architecture and to the site itself. In addition, he brought a particular sensibility to the conditions of the experience that the visitor will have of the garden.

In his design, Irwin integrated the lower slope as an active part of the garden, giving it enough scale to play a strong role. His plan retains the site's natural form as a ravine, into which he incorporated a walkway lined with yarwood sycamores that traverses a small stream edged with a variety of grasses. The walkway descends to a plaza that features arbors of bougainvillea. The stream continues through the plaza, cascading over a stone wall into a pool inset with a maze of azaleas. Surrounding the pool are specialty gardens whose plant material accentuates the interplay of light and reflection.

Irwin selected his materials for their visual qualities, such as pattern, color, texture, and capacity to reflect light. He developed the geometries of the plant material—flowers, leaves, grasses—into large and small forms of the garden. In Irwin's garden, these geometries are compounded by repetition until they are perceived as patterns, and, in turn, patterns are repeated until they are experienced as rich layers of textures.

Irwin conceived the Central Garden as a "conditional" work of art. In contrast to the static, immutable, nature of paintings or sculpture, or even, architecture, Irwin's garden is in flux. His use of seasonal plants and the effects of wind, light, rain, and the shifting sky offer visitors constantly changing experiences conditioned by the hour of day or the time of year.

Harold M. Williams

Bosc of trees
Sceaux, France

Preliminary Plan
August, 1993

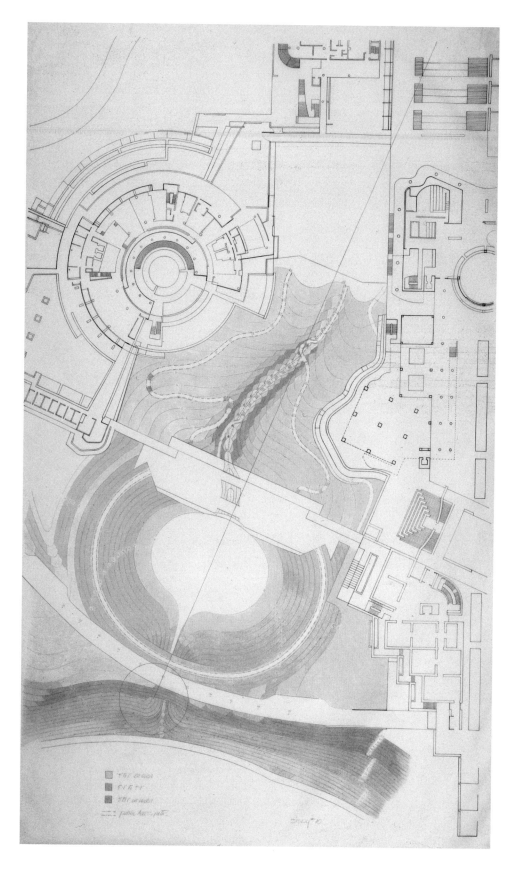

Preliminary Plan
March, 1994

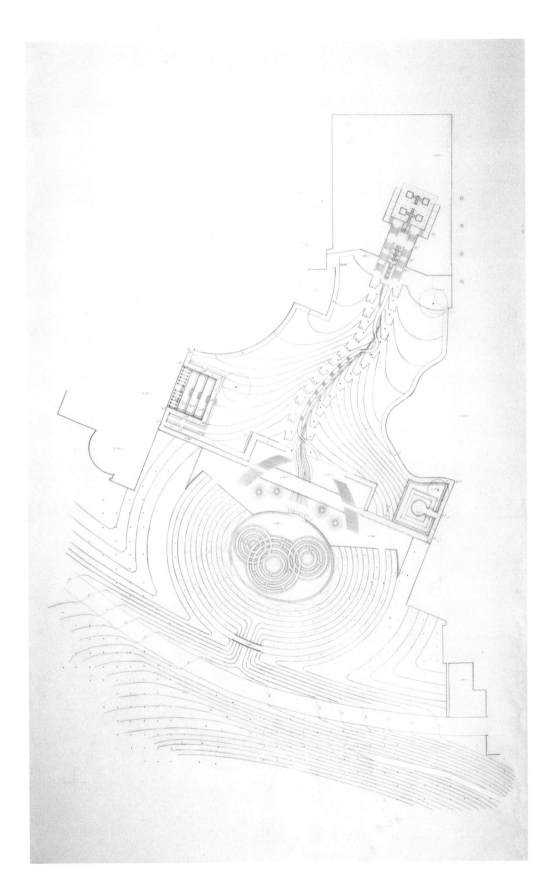

Preliminary Plan
July, 1994

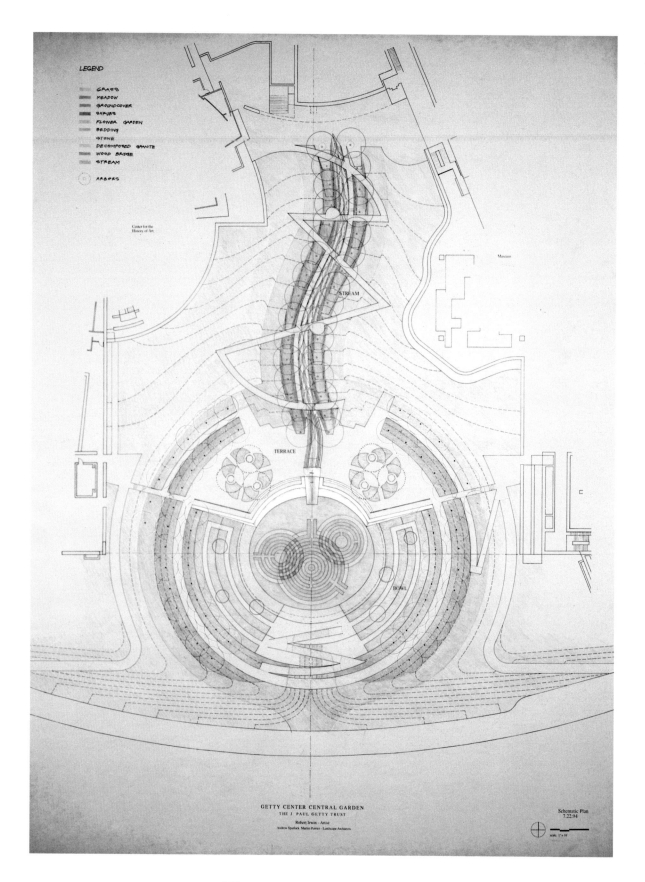

Plant Materials

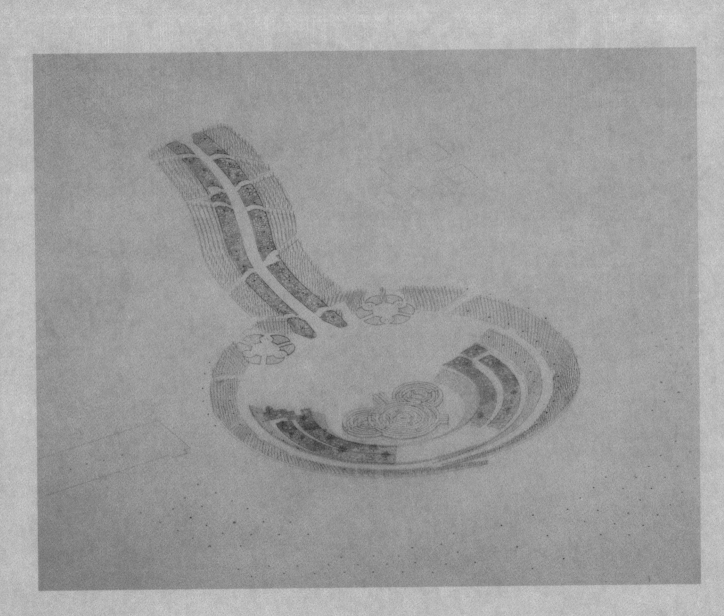

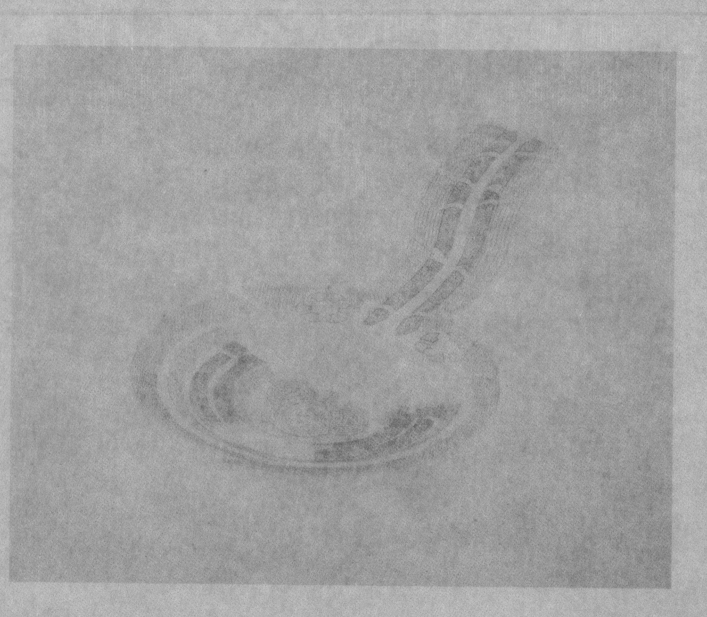

Trees

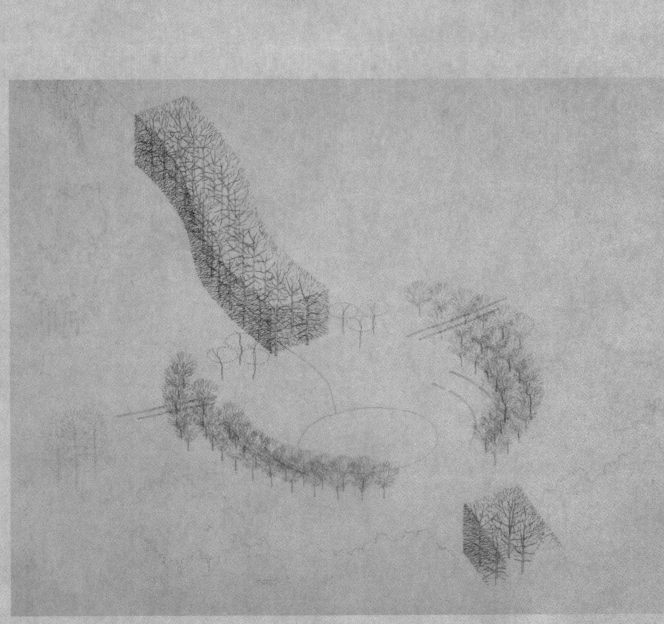

The final plan was rendered as a series of separate drawings
to express the various components of the garden.

Topography
and Built Structures

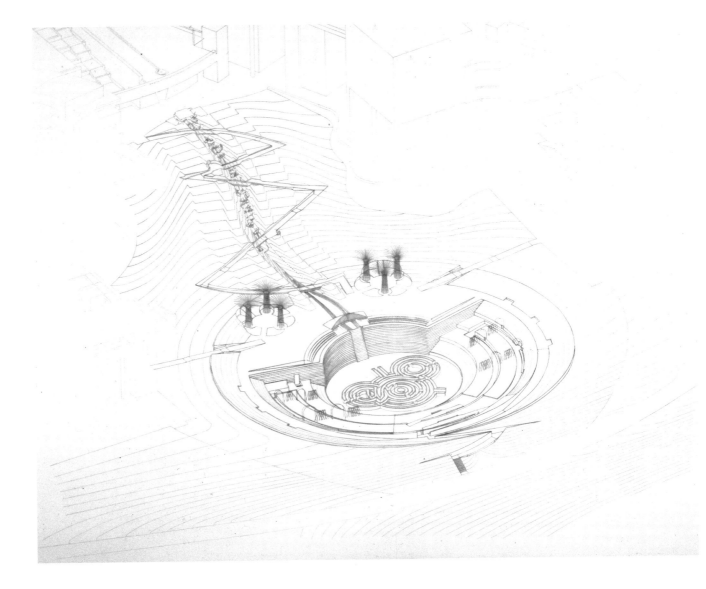

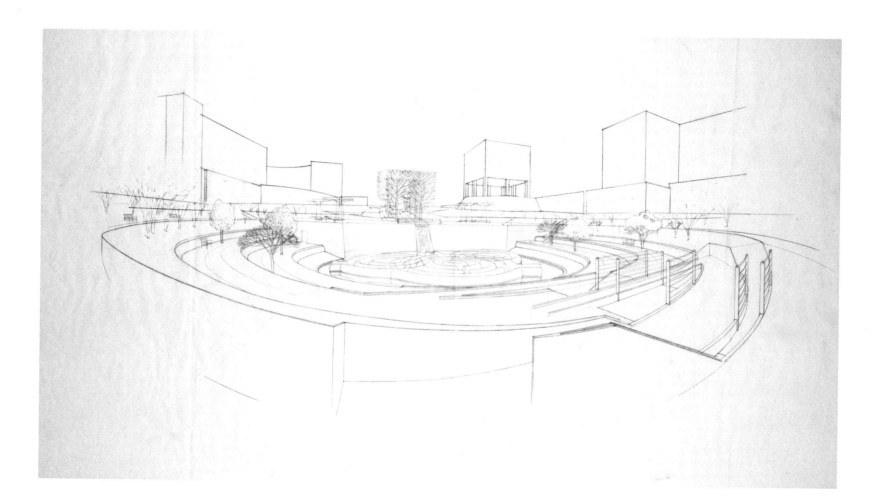

Bougainvillea arbors (*top left*)
Plan view of bougainvillea arbors (*bottom left*)

Azalea maze (*top right*)
Plan view of azalea maze (*bottom right*)

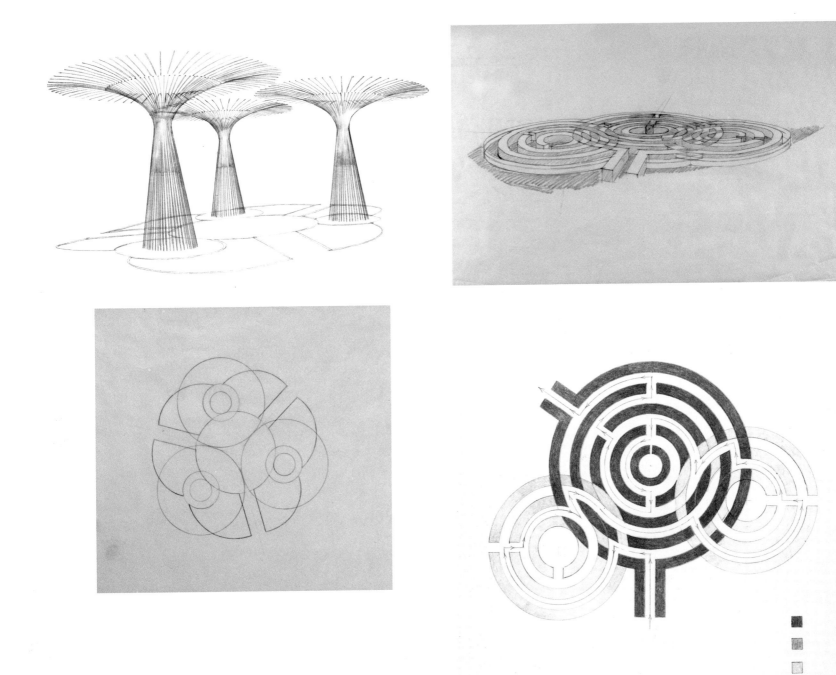

Drawings and photographs
used to study the textures, colors,
and scales of various plant material.

OVERLEAF:
Construction of the Central Garden

PROJECT CREDITS

The Getty Center is the result of the dedicated efforts of hundreds of people; they all should be credited with its success. These pages call out the names of those individuals and firms primarily involved over the past fourteen years.

THE J. PAUL GETTY TRUST
Harold M. Williams
President and Chief Executive Officer

THE J. PAUL GETTY TRUST
BUILDING PROGRAM STAFF
Project Directors
Stephen D. Rountree
Curtis Williams

Project Managers
Monique Birault
Barbara Chiavelli
Charlotte Coulombe
Maria Dion
Georgina Evans
Gloria Gerace
Margaret Jacobson
Elaine Nesbit
Richard Pribnow
Hy Tiano
Timothy Whalen

GETTY PROGRAM DIRECTORS, 1982 TO 1997
Miguel Angel Corzo
Leilani Lattin Duke
Michael Ester
Eleanor Fink
Kurt W. Forster
Deborah Marrow
Luis Monreal
Salvatore Settis
John Walsh

ARCHITECT
Richard Meier & Partners, Architects

Principals-in-Charge
Richard Meier
Michael J. Palladino
Donald E. Barker
James Crawford

Project Architects and Team Leaders
John H. Baker
Tom Graul
Michael Gruber
Dennis Hickok
Richard Kent Irving
Christine Kilian
James Mawson
A. Vic Schnider
Timothy Shea
Richard Stoner
Aram Tatikian
J.F. Warren

GENERAL CONTRACTOR
Dinwiddie Construction Company

Project Directors
Greg Cosko
Peter Mills
Ron Bayek

Project Team Leaders
Bruce Arnold
Gene Frey
Jim Gylling
Jim Hearn
George Irvine
George Kovacic
Tom Rafferty
Cliff Shuch
Rudi Villasenor
Jerry Washington

CENTRAL GARDEN
Robert Irwin
Andrew Spurlock Martin Poirier

GALLERY DESIGN CONSULTING
The Office of Thierry W. Despont, Ltd.

PRIMARY CONSULTANTS

Acoustical Consulting
Paul S. Veneklasen & Associates

Audio/Visual Consulting
Paoletti Associates, Inc.

Civil Engineering
B&E Engineers
RBA Partners, Inc.

Color Consultant
Kaufman/Dahl

Cost Estimating
Hanscomb Associates

Elevators
Hesselberg, Keesee & Associates

Exterior Enclosure Consultants
CDC, Inc.

Fire Protection
Rolf Jensen & Associates, Inc.

Food Service
Cini-Little International

Geotechnical Services
Pacific Soils Engineering, Inc.
Woodward-Cyde Consultants

Laboratory Consultants
Earl Walls Associates

Landscape Architects
Olin Partnership / Fong & Associates
Emmet L. Wemple & Associates
The Office of Dan Kiley

Lighting Design
Fisher Marantz Renfro Stone, Inc.

Mechanical and Electrical Engineering
Altieri Sebor Wieber
Hayakawa Associates

Project Management Consultants
Karsten/Hutman Margolf

Scheduling Consultants
Poulsen Construction Management, Inc.

Specifications
American Nova Co.

Structural Engineering
Robert Englekirk Consulting Structural
Engineers, Inc.

Water Feature Design
CMS Collaborative

PRIMARY SUBCONTRACTORS

Display Cases
Helmut Guenschel, Inc.

Drywall and Plaster, Museum
Raymond-Martin, A Joint Venture

*Drywall and Plaster, North and East Buildings
and Research Institute*
Berger Bros., Inc.

Electrical
Sasco

Elevators
Fujitec

Excavation and Mass Grading
Ebensteiner Company

Exterior Enclosure
Harmon, Ltd.

Heating, Ventilation, and Air Conditioning
Air Conditioning Company, Inc.

Landscape
American Landscape, Inc.
Valley Crest, Inc.

*Millwork—Decorative Arts Galleries
and Research Institute*
Wigand Corporation

Millwork—North and East Buildings and Museum
Brochsteins Inc.

Ornamental Iron
Washington Iron Works

Plumbing
Murray Company

Restoration of French Panels in Two Galleries
Les Ateliers de la Chapelle

Stone
DBM/Hatch Inc.

Tram
Otis Elevator